Teeline
Word List

653.(? HIL

Teeline Word List

I.C.HILL

HEINEMANN
EDUCATIONAL

Heinemann Educational
a division of Heinemann Educational Books Ltd
Halley Court, Jordan Hill, Oxford OX2 8EJ

OXFORD   LONDON   EDINBURGH
MADRID   ATHENS   BOLOGNA   PARIS
MELBOURNE   SYDNEY   AUCKLAND
IBADAN   NAIROBI   HARARE   GABORONE
SINGAPORE   TOKYO   PORTSMOUTH NH (USA)

First published 1981
91 92 93 94 95 21 20 19 18 17 16 15 14 13 12

British Library Cataloguing in Publication Data

Hill, I. C.
   Teeline word list.
   1.   Shorthand – Teeline – Study and teaching
   I. Title
   653'.428   Z56

   ISBN 0-435-45344-0

Other Teeline titles available
Teeline: Revised Edition by I. C. Hill and Meriel Bowers
Teeline Revised Edition: Teacher's Guide by Meriel Bowers
Teeline Fast by Ann Dix
Teeline Shorthand Made Simple by Harry Butler
First Teeline Workbook: Revised Edition by I. C. Hill and Meriel Bowers
Second Teeline Workbook: Revised Edition by I. C. Hill and Meriel Bowers
Teeline Word Groupings by George Hill
New Teeline Dictation Book edited by George Hill
Teeline Shorthand Dictation Passages by Dorothy Bower
Handbook for Teeline Teachers edited by Harry Butler
Medical Teeline by Pat Garner and Pat Clare

Printed in England by Clays Ltd, St Ives plc

CONTENTS

INTRODUCTION

This is a list of common words which does not claim to be comprehensive. However, a study of the outlines should make it possible for any word not included to be written satisfactorily by using the outline of a similar word as a guide and by applying Teeline principles to the longhand.

Where there are alternative outlines, either both are shown, or the one chosen is that which is considered to be the easiest or quickest to write. For instance, PROFESSIONAL can be written either

or

The former outline keeps more strictly to Teeline theory, but the latter avoids splitting the outline into three separate sections, thus reducing writing time.

The writer's own preferred outline may be added if this differs from the one given.

Special contraction of words

Where words are contracted for use in groupings or as word beginnings or endings, this is shown in brackets, as follows:

(g) – in groupings,
(b) – as a word beginning,
(e) – as a word ending.

Examples of these are:

Hundred, which is ⌐ standing alone, but ___ when used in groupings.

Super, which is ⌐ standing alone, but ᴾ when used as a word beginning, and

Word, which is ⌐ standing alone, but ⌐ when used as a word ending or in groupings.

Plurals, past tenses and the addition of ING

As a general rule, plurals are not given, as S can usually be added without any other change of outline, e.g.

_____ link _____ links

_____ comrade _____ comrades

Where a change is required, the plural is usually shown, e.g.

_____ bus _____ buses

_____ country _____ countries

The plural is also given where it forms a distinctive outline with a similar word, e.g. adventures and adventurous, or where the plural is more commonly (or as commonly) used as the singular, e.g. after-effects, barracks, things, etc.

Similarly, the addition of D to show the past tense, or ING, will not usually be given. These signs can easily be added to the outline, e.g.

_____ act _____ acted _____ acting.

LY ending

This may often be contracted by omitting the L, e.g.

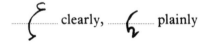

_____ clearly, _____ plainly

although there are a few cases where the inclusion of L is necessary to avoid confusion or hesitation in reading back, e.g.

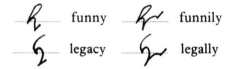

_____ funny _____ funnily

_____ legacy _____ legally

NT ending

N may often be omitted with safety, e.g.

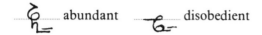

abundant   disobedient

The addition of vowels to word endings

Vowels may be added to disjoined word endings if required, for easier reading back, e.g.

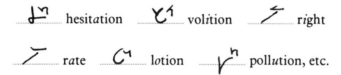

hesitation   volition   right

rate   lotion   pollution, etc.

Outlines are of course equally correct without the addition of such vowels.

NCH ending

As a disjoined C is used for the NC ending, it was thought logical to use a disjoined CH for the NCH ending. This has been introduced in *Teeline: Revised Edition* and is given in this list. It may prove to be an acceptable alternative to the NCH blend previously used.

JECT ending

There are not many of these and two of them—subject and object—have been used in their contracted forms in the textbook *Teeline: Revised Edition.* In the words inject and reject it is easier to disjoin the J. This method of contracting considerably shortens the outline.

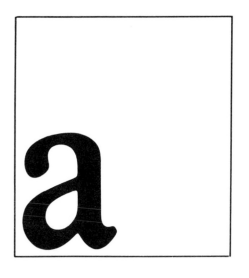

a

abandon

abate

abatement

abbey

abbreviate

abbreviation

ability (e)

able (e)

ably (e)

abnormal or

abnormality or

abolish

abolition

about or

above (b)

abroad

absence or

absent

absentee

absenteeism

absolute

absolutely or

absorb

abstain

abstainer

abstract

absurd

abundance

abundant

abundantly

abuse

abused or

academic

academy

accept	accuse
acceptance	accused
accessible	ache ... or
accessories	achieve
accident/al ... X ... /	achievement
acclaim	acknowledge ... or
acclamation	acknowledgement ... or
accommodate	acoustics ... or
accommodation	acquaint
accompaniment	acquaintance
accompany	acquire
accomplish	acquired
accomplishment	acquisition
accordance	across
according	act
accordingly	action
accountant ... or	active
account/s ... or ... / ... or	activity
accuracy ... or	actor
accurate	actress/es ... /
accurately	actual

actuality	administer ... or ...
actuary	administrate ... or ...
acumen	administration ... or ...
acute	administrator ...
acutely	admirable ...
adapt	admire ...
adaptable	admirer ...
adaptation	admit ...
add	admittance ...
added	admitted ...
adequate	admittedly ...
adequately	adopt ...
addict	adorable ...
addition	adorably ...
additional	adrenalin ...
additives	adult ...
address	advance ...
adjudicate	advantage ...
adjudicator	advantageous ...
adjust	advantages ...
adjustment	adventure/s ... / ...

adventurous

advertise

advertiser

advertisement

advertising ... or ...

advice ... or ...

advisable

advise

advisory

aerate ... or ...

aerial

aerobatics

aerodrome

aerodynamics

aeroplane

aerosol

aesthetic

affair

affect ... or ...

affectation ... or ...

affection ... or ...

affectionately ... or ...

afield

afford

afraid

after ... (b) ... (e)

after-dinner

after-effects

aftermath

afternoon

afterthought ... or ...

afterwards

again

against

age

agency

agenda

agent

aggression

aggressive

agile

agility

ago	alcohol
agony/ies /	alderman
agreeable	aldermen
agree/d /	ale
agreement or	alert or
agricultural	all
agriculture	allay
aid	allegation
ail	allege
aim	allergy
aimless	alley
air or (b)	allocate
aircraft	allocation
airiness	allot or
airless	allow
airman	allowance
airmen	alloy
airport	ally
airy or	almost
aisle	alms or
album or	alone

along

alongside

alphabet

already

also

alter

alteration

alternate

alternately

alternative

alternatively

although

altogether

aluminium

always

am

amalgamate

amalgamation

amateur

amazed ... or ...

ambassador

ambition

ambitious

amble

ambulance

amenable

amend

amendment

amenity

American

among

amongst

amount ... or ...

ample

amplified

amplifier

amplify

amuse

amusement

an

anagram

analysis ... or ...

analyst ... *or* ...

ancient ...

and ...

angle ...

angrily ...

angry ...

animal ...

annex ...

annihilate ...

anniversary ...

announce/d ... / ...

announcement ...

announcer ...

annoy ...

annoyance ...

annual ...

another ...

answer/ed ... / ...

antacid ...

antagonism ...

antagonize ...

antagonist ...

antagonistic ...

antecedent ...

antedate ...

antelope ...

ante-room ...

anthem ... *or* ...

anthropologist ...

anthropology ...

antibiotics ...

antibody ...

anticipate ...

anticipation ...

anticlimax ...

anti-clockwise ...

anticyclone ...

antidote ...

antipathetic ...

antipathy ...

antipodes ...

antiquated ...

antique	appear/ance
antiquity	append
antiseptic	appendicitis
anti-social	appendix
anxiety	appetite
anxious	applaud
anxiously	applause
any	apple
anyone	appliance
anybody	applicable
anything	applicant
anyway	application
anywhere	applied
apartment	apply
apathetic	appoint
apathy	appointment
apparatus	apportion
apparent/ly	appreciate
ape	appreciation
apex	apprehensive
appeal	apprentice

apprenticeship

approach

appropriate

approval

approve

approximate/ly

apricot

April

apron

apropos

apt

aquatic

arbitrate

arbitration

arbitrator

arch ... or ...(b)

archaeologist

archaeology

archangel

archbishop

archduke

architect

architectural

architecture

are

area/s

argue

argument

argumentative

arise/n

arm

army

around ... or ...

arrange

arrangement

array

arrival

arrive

art

arthritic ... or ...

arthritis

article

artificial

artificiality

artisan

artist

artistic

artistically

as

ascertain ... or ...

ashamed

ask ... or ...

asked

asleep

aspect/s ... / ...

asperity

assassin

assassination ... or ...

assault/ed ... / ...

assemble

assembly

assess/ment ... / ...

assiduous ... or ...

assist

assistance

assistant ... or ...

associate

association ... or ... (g)

assume

assurance

assure/d ... / ...

astray

astrologer

astrology

astronaut

astronomer

astronomy

at

ate

atom

atomic ... (g)

attach

attack/er ... / ...

attempt

attend

attendance

attention ... or

attire

attitude ... or

attraction

attractive

auction

audible

audience

August

aunt

author

authoritative

authority ... or ... (g)

authorize ... or

auto ... (b)

autocrat

autograph

automated

automatic

automatically

automation

automobile

autopsy

autumn

avail/able ... /

avenue

average

averse

aversion

avoid

await

awake

aware

awareness

awash

away

awe

awful

awkward ... or

axe

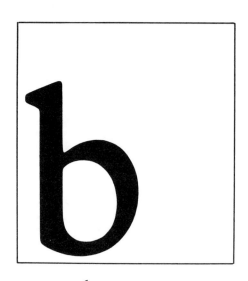

baby

bachelor

back

background

backlog

backwards

bacon

bad/ly

baffle

bag

baggage

bake   or

baker

bakery

balance

ball

ballet

balloon

ballpoint

ban

band

bandit

bang

bangle

bank

banker

banking

bankrupt

bankruptcy

banned

banns

banquet

bar/bare   or

barely   or

bark

barracks

barred

barrel

barren

barrier _____ or _____

base

bash

basic

basis

bask

basket

bat

bath/bathe

bathroom

battle

bay

bazaar _____ or _____

be

beach

bear/er _____ / _____

beard

beat

beautiful/ly _____ / _____

beauty

became

because

become

bed

bedlam

bedroom _____ or _____

bedside _____ or _____

bedsitter

bee/s _____ / _____

beef

been _____ or _____ (g)

before

beforehand

began

beggar

begin

beginner

behalf

behave	bestow
behaviour	bet/ter /
behind	between
being	bewilder
belief _or_	bewitch
believe	beyond
belong	bias/ed /
below	Bible
bench _or_	bid/bide
bend	big/bigger /
beneficial	biggest
beneficiary	bi-lingual
benefit	bill
benevolence	billow
benevolent	bin
bequeath	bingo _or_
bequest	biographer
berry	biography
beset	biological
beside	biologist
best	biology

bird

birth

birthday

biscuit

bit/bite

black/er

blackest

blame

blanch

blank

blanket

blare

blaze

blend

blender

blew

block

bloom

blossom

blue

blunder

blunt

bluster

blustery

board

boardroom

boat

body

boil

bomb

bombard

bond

bondage

bone

bonfire

bonus/es

boo

book

boon

boost

boot/s

bored

boredom	Braille
born	brain
borough	brainwashed _or_
borrow/er /	branch _or_
both	brand
bother	brand-new
bottle	brandy
bottom	brass
bough	brave
bought	bravely
bounce	bravery
bounced	breach
bound	bread
boundary	breadcrumbs
bowl	break
box _or_	breakdown
boxer	breakfast
boy/buoy	breath/breathe
boyhood	breeze _or_
boyish	brevity _or_
bra	brick

bridge	broth
brief _or_	brother
brief-case	brought _or_
brigade	brown
bright	brush _or_
brighten	brushes _or_
brilliance	brutal
brilliant	brutality
bring	brutally
Britannia	brute
British	bubble
Briton	bubbly
brittle	bucket
broad	budget
broadcast	buff
brochure _or_	build
broke/n /	builder
broker	bulk
bronchitis _or_	bull
bronze	bulldozer
bros.	bulletin

bump	burst
bumper	bury
bunch _or_	bus/es _or_ / _or_
bundle	bush/es /
bunk	bushy
bunker	business
bureau	businessman _or_
bureaucracy _or_	busy
bureaucrat _or_	but
bureaucratic _or_	butcher
burglar	butter
burgle	button
buried	buyer
burly	by/buy
burn	bygone

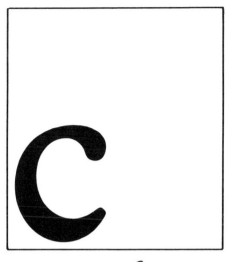

camber	
came	
camel	
camera	
camp/er	/
campaign	
can	
cab or	cancel or
cabbage	cancellation or
cabinet	candidate or
cable	candy
cactus	cannot
cadence	can't
cadet or	canvas
cage	capability
cake	capable
call or	capably
caller	capacious
calligraphy	capacity
calm	capital
calmness	capitalize

capitation

captain

caption

captive

car

caravan

card

cardiograph

care

career ... or

careful/ly ... /

careless/ly ... /

carelessness

caretaker

cargo

car park ... or

carpet

carriage

carry

carve

case

cash

catalogue

catch

category ... or

caught

cause

caution

cautionary

cave

cavity

cease

celebrate

celebration

cemetery

censor ... or

cent

centenarian

centenary

centimetre

central

centre

century ____ or ____ (g)	Chancellor
cereal	Chancellor of the Exchequer
certain	change
certainly	changeable
certainty	changeless
certificate	changeover
certified	channel
certify	chap
cervix	chapel
cessation	chapter
chain	character
chair	characteristic
chairman	charge
chalk ____ or ____	charity
chalkboard ____ or ____	charm
challenge	chart
challenger	charter
chamber	chase
Chamber of Commerce	chatter
champagne	chauffeur
chance/d ____ / ____	cheap

check		childhood	
check-out	or	children	
cheek		chill/y	/
cheeky	or	chimes	
cheer		chimney	
cheerful/ly	/	Chinese	
cheerfulness		chisel	
cheerless		chocolate	
cheerlessness		choice	or
cheese		choke/d	/
chef		chop	
chemical		chopsticks	
chemist		choral	or
chemistry		chore	
cheque		chorus	
cherry		chosen	
chest		Christmas	or
chew		chubby	
chicken		chuck	
child		chug	
childbirth		chum	

church

churlish/ly

cider

cigar

cigarette

cinder

cinema/s

circle

circuit

circular

circulate

circulation

circumcise

circumcision

circumference

circumscribe

circumspect

circumstance

circumstantial

circumvent

circus

citizens

city .... or .... (g)

civil

civilized

civic

claim

clap

clarification .... or ....

clarify .... or ....

class

classic/al

classified .... or ....

classify .... or ....

classroom

clause

clay

clean

cleaner

clear

clearer

clearing

clearly		coast	
clerk	or	coat	
clever/ly	/	cobble	co
cliché		cobweb	
client		cocoa	
clientele		cocktail	
climate		codicil	or
climb		coexist	or
clinch	or	coexistence	or
cling		coffee	or
clock		coherence	
close		coherent	or
closure		coincide	or
cloth/clothe		coincidence	or
cloud	or	cold/er	/
clown		collar	
club		colleague	
clue		collect/or	/
clutter		collection	
coal		college	
coarse		colony	

colour/ful .... / ....

comb ....

combat ....

combination ....

combine/d .... / ....

combustible ....

combustion .... or ....

come ....

comfort ....

comfortable ....

comic/al .... / ....

command/er .... / ....

commandment ....

commence ....

commencement ....

commend ....

commendable ....

comment ....

commerce .... or ....

commercial/ly .... / ....

commemorate ....

commemoration ....

commission ....

commissioner ....

commit ....

committee .... or .... (g)

commodity ....

common ....

commonplace ....

commonsense ....

communicate ....

communication ....

communique ....

community ....

commuter ....

companion ....

company .... or .... (g)

comparative/ly .... / ....

comparison ....

compass ....

compatible ....

compel ....

compensate	comprehend
compensation	comprehensive
competent	compress
competition or	compression
competitive	compromise
competitors	compulsory
compile	compute
complacent	computer
complain	computerized
complainant	comrade
complained	comradeship
complaint	conceal or
complement	concentrate
complementary	concentration
complete	concept or
complex	conception or
compliment	concern or
complimentary	concert or
comply	concrete
compose	concur
compost or	concurrence

concussion		confirmation	
condemn		conflict	
condemnation		confuse	
condensation		confusion	
condense		congratulate	
condition		congratulations	
conditional		conjure	
condone		conjurer	
conduct		connect	
conductor		connection	
confederation		connivance	
confer		connive	
conference		connoisseur	
confess/ion		conquer	
confessional		conscientious	
confidence		conscious/ly	
confident		consecrate	
confidential		consequence	
confine		consequent/ly	
confinement		consensus	
confirm		conservation	

conservative

conserve

consider

considerable

considerably

consideration

consign/ment

consist

consistent/ly

consolidate

consolidation

conspicuous

conspicuously

constant/ly

constituency

constituent

constitute

constitution

construct/ion

constructive

consult

consultancy

consultant

consume

consumer

consumption

contact

contain/er

contaminate

contamination

contemporary

contempt

content

contention

contest

continent

continental

continual/ly

continuance

continue

continuous

continuously

contortion	convenience
contract	convenient ... or
contraction	conveniently ... or
contradict	convent
contradiction	convention
contralto	converge
contrary	conversation
contravene	converse
contravention	convert
contribute	convey
contribution	conveyance
contrition	convict
contrivance	conviction
contrive	convince
control	convivial
controversial	cook/ed ... /
controversy	cooker
convalesce	cookery
convalescent ... or	cool/er ... /
convene	co-operate
convener	co-operation

co-ordinate		cottage	
co-ordination		cotton	
copper		cough	or
copy		could	
copyright		council	or ... (g)
cord		councillor	or
cork		counsel	
corn		counsellor	
corner		count	
coroner		countenance	or
corporation	or	counter	(b)
correct		counterfeit	
correction		counterfoil	
correspond		counterpart	
correspondence		countries	
correspondingly		country	
corridor		countryside	or
corroboration		county	
corroborative		couple	
cost		coupon	
costly	or	course	

court	create ... or
courteous ... or	creation
courtesy	creative ... or
cousin	credit
cover	creditor
cow	crew
coward/ly ... /	crime
cox	criminal/s ... /
coy	cringe
crab	cripple
crack ... or	crisis ... or
cracker ... or	critic
cradle	critical/ly ... /
craft/y ... /	criticism
craftsman	criticize ... or
crag	crop ... or
crane	cross ... or
crank	crossed ... or
crash ... or	cross-examination
crave	cross-examine
cream	cross-over

crossroads		curb	
crossword		curd	
crowd		curiosity	
crown		curious	
crucial/ly		currency	
crude		current	
cruel		curry	
cruelty		curtail	
cruise		curtain/s	
crumb		curve	
crumble		cushion	
crush		custody	
crutch		custom	
cry		customary	
culprit		customer	
cultivate		cut	
cultivation		cycle	
cultural		cyclist	
culture		cynic	
cumulative		cynical	
cup		cynicism	

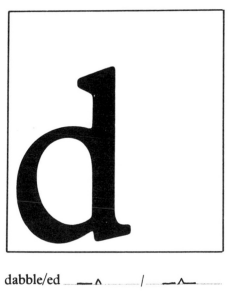

dabble/ed

Dad

daffodil

dahlia

dairy

damage

dance

dancer

danger

dangerous/ly

dare

dark

darkness

darling

darn

dash

date

daub

daughter

daunting

dawn

day

daylight   or

dead/en

deadline

deadly

deaf/en

deal

dealt

dear/er

dearest

death

debate

debentures

debility

debit	deepen
debt/or	defame
decade	defeat
deceased	defective
deceit	defence
deceitful	defenceless
December	defend
decibels	defendant
decide	defensive
decidedly	defer
decision	deference
decisive	deferential
deck	defiance
declaration	defiant
declare	deficiency
decorate	deficient
decorations	deficit
deduce	define/d
deduct	definite
deduction	definitely
deep	degradation

degrade

degree

deity

delay

delegate

deliberate/ly

delicacy or

delicate

delicious or

delight

delightful

delinquency

delinquent

deliver/y /

deluge

demand

democracy or

democrat

democratic

democratically

demolish or

demonstrate

demonstration or

dent

dentist

deny

depart

department

departure

depend

dependant/ent /

deplete

deplorable

deplore

deploy

deposit

deprave

depravity

deprecate

depreciate

depreciation

depress

deprivation	destruction
deprive	destructive
depth	detach
deputy	detachment
derelict	detail
describe	detain
description	detect
descriptive	detective
desert	detention
deserve	deter
design	deteriorate ... or ...
desirable	deterioration
desire	determination
desk	determine
despair	deterrent
despicable	detest/able ... / ...
despise	detriment/al ... / ...
destination	detour
destined	develop ... or ...
destiny	development
destroy	devil

devote

devotion

devour

dexterity

dexterous

diagram

dial

diamonds

diary

dice

Dictaphone

dictate

dictator

dictionary

did

die

diet

differ

difference

different/ly

differential

differentiation

difficult/y

diffidence

diffident

dig

digest

dignity

diligence

diligent/ly

dim

dimension

diminution

dining

dinner

dip

diploma

diplomat

direct

direction

director

directory

dirty	discreet
disabled	discrepancy
disadvantage	discretion
disagree/ment /	discriminate
disappoint/ment /	discrimination
disapproval	discuss/ion /
disapprove	disease
disaster	disgrace or
disastrous	disgraceful or
discard	disgracefully or
discern or	dish
discharge	dishonest
discipline or	dislike
disclose	dislodge
disclosure	disobedience
discomfort or	disobedient
discontinue	disorder
disco	disorderly
discount or	disparity
discourteous or	dispensary
discover/y /	dispense

display		district	
displeased		disturb	
displeasure		disturbance	
dispose		disused	
disproof		ditch	
disproportionate		dive	
disprove		diversion	
dispute		divert	
disqualified		divide	
disrupt/ion		dividend	(g)
distance		division	
distant		divorce	or
distasteful		divorcee	or
distinct/ly		do	
distinguish/ed		dock	
distract		doctor	
distraction		doctrinaire	
distrain		doctrine	
distress		document	
distribute		documentary	
distribution		documentation	

does	dozen
dog	draft
dogmatic	drag
dogmatism	drain
doing	drank
dollar	draughty
dominion	draw
donation	drawer
done	drawn
door	dread
dot	dreadful/ly
double ... or	dream
double-glazing	dreamer
doubt	dreamily
doubtful ... or	dreamy
doubtless ... or	dress/es /
dough	dresser
down	dried
downpour	drill
downstairs	drink/er /
downward	drive/r /

dromedary

drown

drop

drug

drum

drunk

drunkard

drunken

dry

duck

due

dumb

duplicate

duplicator

durable

during

dusk

dust

dutiful ... or ...

duty ... or ...

dwindle

dye

dyed ... or ...

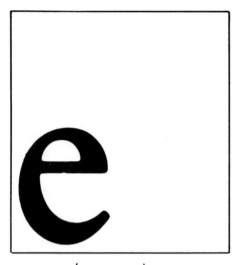

each .... ૬ ..... or ..... ઈ

eager/ly .... ½ ..... / ..... ⅍

ear ..... ✓

earlier ..... ✓í

earliest ..... ✓ɭ

early ..... ✓ɭ

ear-ring ..... ✓′

earth ..... ✓⌐ ..... or ..... ✓⌐

earthquake ..... ✓ɭ ..... or ..... ✓ɭ

earwig ..... ✓⥾

ease ..... b

easier ..... ʋ ..... or ..... ✓

easily ..... ɓ
ʑ ..... ⅃

east

Easter ..... ⅃

eastward ..... ⅃

easy ..... b

eat/en ..... ⌐ ..... / ..... ⌐

eclipse ..... ⅗

ecology ..... ⌐˘

economic/al ..... ⅌ɭ ..... / ..... ⅌ɭ

economics ..... ⅌ɭ

economies ..... ⅌ɭ

economize ..... ⅌ɭ

economy ..... ⅌ʋ

ecstasy ..... ✗ρ

eczema ..... ✗ʍ

edge ..... ɦ

edible ..... ⌐ʋ

edify ..... ⅂ʒ

edit ..... ⌐ ..... or ..... ⌐

edition ..... ⌐ʌ

editor ..... ⌐

editorial ..... ⌐ʒ

educate ..... ⌐ɭ

education/al _____ / _____

effect _____

effective _____

effectively _____

efficiency _____

efficient/ly _____ / _____

effort _____

effortless _____

egg/s _____ / _____

eight _____ or 8

either _____

elastic _____ or _____

elasticity _____ or _____

elated _____

elation _____

elbow _____

elder/ly _____ / _____

elect _____

election _____

electric _____ or _____ (b)

electrical _____ or _____

electrician _____

electricity _____

electrocute _____ or _____

electrode _____

electrolysis _____

electron _____ or _____

electronic _____ or _____

electroplate _____

element _____

elemental _____

elementary _____

elephant _____

elevate _____

eligible _____

eliminate _____

elimination _____

elm _____

elocution _____

eloquence _____

else _____

embankment _____

embarrass

embassy

embroidery

emerge

emergency

eminent/ly /

emission

emotion or

emotionally or

empathy

emphasize or

emphatic/ally /

employ

employee or

employer

employment

empty

enable

enact

enchant

encircle

enclose

enclosure

encompass

encore

encounter

encourage

encouragement

encroach

encumbrance

encyclopaedia

end

endeavour

endless/ly /

enemy

energetic

energy

enforce/ment /

engage/ment /

engine

engineer

English

engraving

enjoy ... or

enjoyment ... or

enough

enormous/ly ... /

enquire/s ... /

enquiries ... or

enquiry ... or

enrol

enrolment

ensure

enter/s ... /

enterprise

entertain

entertainer

entertainment

enthuse ... or

enthusiasm ... or

enthusiastic ... or

enthusiastically ... or

entire/ly ... /

entitled

entrance

entries

entry

envelope

environment

epic

episode

epoch

equal

equality

equate

equation

equip

equipment

equitable

equities

equivalent

errand

erratic

error

erudite		eventual/ly	/
erupt/ion	/	eventuality	
escape		ever	or ..... (b)
especial/ly	/	evergreen	
essential/ly	/	ever-increasing	
establish		everlasting	
establishment		ever-loving	
estate		evermore	
estimate		every	or
etching		everybody	or
etymology		everyone	or
Europe		everything	or
European		everywhere	or
evacuate		evict	
evacuation		eviction	
evade		evidence	or ..... (g)
evaluate		evident/ly	/
eve		evil	
even		evolution	
evening		evolve	
event		ewe	

ewer	exchequer ... or
exact	excise
exactly ... or	excite ... or
exam.	excitedly ... or
examination	excitement ... or
examine/r ... /	exclaim
example	exclamation
excavate	exclude
excavations	exclusive/ly ... /
exceed	excruciating
exceeding/ly ... /	excursion
excel ... or	excuse
excellent ... or	executive ... or
except	executor
exception	exempt ... or
exceptional/ly ... /	exercise/s ... /
excess	exert/ion ... /
excessive/ly ... /	exhaust/ion ... /
execrable	exhibit/ion ... /
excerpt ... or	exhibitionist
exchange	exhort

exist

existence

exorbitant ... or ...

exorcise

exorcist

exotic ... or ...

expand

expanse

expansion

expect

expectations

expedition

expeditionary

expel

expend

expenditure

expense

expensive

experience

experiment

experimental/ly ... / ...

expert

expire

explain

explanation

explanatory

explode

exploit

exploration

explore

explosion

explosive

export/er ... / ...

expose

exposure

express

expression

expressive

expropriate

expulsion

extend

extension

extensive/ly ... / ...

extent ...

external/ly ... / ...

extinct ...

extinguish ...

extinguisher ...

extortionate ...

extra ...

extract ...

extraction ...

extradition ... or ...

extraordinary ...

extravagance ...

extravagant ...

extravaganza ... or ...

extreme/ly ... / ...

extricate ...

extrovert ...

eye/s ... / ...

eyeing ...

eyesight ...

fable

fabric

fabulous

face ... or ... or

facet ... or

facial

facile ... or

facility

fact

factor

factory

factual

faculty

fail

failure

faint ... or

fair

fairground ... or

fairly

fairness

faith

faithful

faithfully

fake

fall/en ... /

false/ly ... /

familiar ... or

familiarity ... or

familiarization ... or

family

famous

famously

fan

fancied ... or

fancy ... or

fangs	fault/y	
far	favour/able	
farce _or_	favoured	
fares	favourite	
farm	fear/ful	
farmer	feasible	
far-off	feast	
farther	feather	
fascinate _or_	feature	
fascination _or_	February	
fashion	feckless	
fashionable	fed	
fashionably	fee _or_	
fast/er	feeble	
fastest	feed	
fatal/ly	feel/ings	
fatality	feelingly	
fateful	feet	
father	fell	
fathom	fellow	
fatuous	fellowship	

felony	fidelity
felt	fidget
female	field
feminine	fierce _or_
fence	fiery
fend	fifth
ferry	fig
fertile	fight
fertility	figure
festive	file
festivity	fill
fetch	film
feud	final _or_
feudal	finalist _or_
few/er	finality _or_
fibres	finance
fibrous	financial
fibula	find
fickle _or_	fine
fiction _or_	finger
fictional _or_	fingertips

finish — *[shorthand]* or *[shorthand]*

fire — *[shorthand]*

fireplace — *[shorthand]* or *[shorthand]*

firewood — *[shorthand]*

firm — *[shorthand]*

firmly — *[shorthand]* or *[shorthand]*

firmness — *[shorthand]*

first — *[shorthand]*

first-class — *[shorthand]*

fiscal — *[shorthand]*

fish — *[shorthand]*

fisherman — *[shorthand]*

fit/ter — *[shorthand]* / *[shorthand]*

fitting/ly — *[shorthand]* / *[shorthand]*

five — *[shorthand]*

fix — *[shorthand]* or *[shorthand]*

fixative — *[shorthand]* or *[shorthand]*

fixture — *[shorthand]*

flag — *[shorthand]*

flame — *[shorthand]*

flan — *[shorthand]*

flank — *[shorthand]*

flash — *[shorthand]* or *[shorthand]*

flat — *[shorthand]*

flat-iron — *[shorthand]*

flavour — *[shorthand]* or *[shorthand]*

flew — *[shorthand]*

flex/ible — *[shorthand]* / *[shorthand]*

flexibility — *[shorthand]*

flinch — *[shorthand]* or *[shorthand]*

fling — *[shorthand]*

float — *[shorthand]*

flood — *[shorthand]* or *[shorthand]*

floor — *[shorthand]*

flounce — *[shorthand]*

flourish — *[shorthand]*

flower — *[shorthand]*

flowerbeds — *[shorthand]*

fluctuate — *[shorthand]*

fluctuation — *[shorthand]*

fly/er — *[shorthand]* / *[shorthand]*

flyover — *[shorthand]*

focus	forest
focused	foresee/able
foe	foreword
fog/gy	forfeit/ure
fold	forget
folk	forgive/n
follow	forgot/ten
fond	fork
fondness	form
food	formal
fool	formality
foolish	formally
foot	formation
for	former/ly
forbear	formidable
forbearance	fort
force/ful	forth
forcefully	fortunate
foregoing	fortune
foreign	forty
foreigner	forum

forward	fresh/en
found	fresheners
foundation	freshness
founder	Friday
four	fridge
fowl	friend/ship
fraction	frieze
fragment	fright/en
fragmentary	frightful/ness
frame	fringe
frank/ed	frivolity
frankly	frivolous
frantic/ally	frog
fraud	from
free	front
freedom	frost/y
freehold	frown/ed
freeze	frozen
freight	fruit
French	fruitful
frequent/ly	fruitfulness

fuel		fur	
fulfil		furnish	
fulfilment		furniture	
full/er	/	furry	
fully		further/ance	/
fumble		furthermore	
fume/s	/	fuss/y	/
fun	or	futile	
function	or	future	
funds		futility	
funfair		fuzzy	
funny	or		

gadget

gain

gale _or_

gallant

galleon

gallery _or_

gallon

gamble

game

gang

garage

garb

garbage

garden/er /

gargle _or_

garment

gas _or_

gate

gather

gauge

gave

gay

gaze

gazette _or_

genealogy

general

generalize _or_

generalization

generally

generate

generation

generosity

generous _or_

generously _or_

genteel

gentle	Girobank
gentleman ... or	girt
gentlemen ... or	give/n ... /
genuine	glad/ly ... /
geographical	glance
geography	glass/es ... /
geologist/geology ... /	glimpse
geometry	glorious
germ/s ... /	glove
German	glow
germinate	glutton/y ... /
gesture/s ... /	go ... or
get	goal
ghastly	goat
gift	gobble/d ... /
giggle	goblet
ginger	god
gingerbread	gold/en ... /
gird/er ... /	good
girl/ish ... /	good-bye
giro	good-natured

goodness	graphite	
goodnight	graphologist	
goodwill	graphology	
gorge	grapple	
gospel	grasp	
gossip	grass	or
govern	grateful	
government	gratitude	or
grab	grave	
grace	gravity	
grade	great/er	/
gradual/ly	/	greatest	
graduate/ed	/	greed/ily	/
grain	greedy	
gram	or	(e)	Greek	or
gramophone	green	or
grand	grew	
grandfather	or	grey	
grandmother	grid	
grant	or	grievance	or
graph	or	(e)	grim/e	

grip

grocer

grocery

gross/ly /

ground/less /

group

grow

growl

grown

growth

grudge

gruff/ly /

grumble

guarantee

guard

guardian

guess

guest

guide

guild

guilt/y / or

guinea

gullible

gullibility

gulp

gun

gush

gust

gusto

guy

gymnast

gymnastics

gynaecology

gypsy

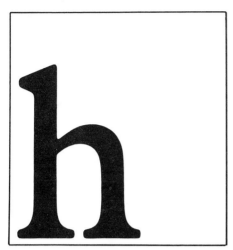

habit

hackneyed

had

haggle

hair

hake k or

half

hall

halt

hammer

hamper

hand

handbag

handle

handy

handwriting

hang

hangover

hank

happen

happily

happiness

happy

harbour

hard/ly

hardship

hardy

harm

harmful or

harmless

harmonious

harmony

harsh/ness

harvest

has

hasty		heard	
hat ... or		heart/y ... /	
hatch		heat/ing ... /	
hate		heath	
hatred		heat-stroke	
have		heat wave	
haven		heaven/ly ... /	
hay		heavily	
hazard ... or		heavy	
haze		hedge	
hazy		hedgehog ... or	
he		hefty	
head		held	
headache		hello	
headlines		helm ... or	
headquarters		help/ful ... /	
headway		helpless	
health		hen	
healthiest		hence	
healthy		henceforth ... or	
hear		her	

herb	hint/s
here	hire
hereafter	hire purchase
herewith	his
herself _or_	historic/al
hesitate	history
hesitation	hit
hexagon	hitherto
hibernate	hoard
hibernation _or_	hobble
hid/den	hobby
hi-fi	hockey
high/er	hold
hi-jack	hole
highlight	holiday
high-speed	hollow
hilarious _or_	home/less
hilarity	homely _or_
hill	home-made
him	homeopathic
himself _or_	homeopathy

honest/ly	hospital
honey	hospitality
honour/ed	host
honourable	hostile
hood	hostility
hook	hot
hoop	hotel
hop	hotter
hope	hour ... or
hopeful/ly	house ... or
hopeless	housebreaking
hopelessness	household
horizon	housewife
horn	how
horrible	however ... or
horribly	howl
horror	hug
horse	huge
horse-drawn	human
hose	humanity
hospitable	humble/ness

humiliate

humiliation

humility

humorous

humour

hundred ... *or* ____ (g)

hung

hungrily

hungry

hunt/er ... /

hurry

hurt

husband

hush

husk

hutch

hygiene

hymn

hyperactive

hyperactivity

hyperbole

hypermobility

hypertension

hypocrisy

hypocrite

hypocritical

hypodermic

hypotenuse

hypothermia

hypothesis

hypothetical

I

ice

ice cream

icicles

idea/s   /

ideal

idle

idolize

idols

if

igloo

ignite

ignition

ignorance

ignore

ill

illness

illuminate

illuminations

illustrate

illustrations

image

imaginary

imagination

imagine

immaterial

immediate/ly   /

immersion

immune

immunization

immunize

imp

impair

impart

impartial   s

impartiality

impassioned

impatience

impatient/ly

imperial

impermeable

impersonation

impertinence

impertinent

imperturbable

implement

implementation

imply

import

importance

important/ly

importer

impossible

impracticable

impregnate

impresario

impress

impression/able

impressive

improbable/ably

improper/ly

improve

improvement

imprudent

impulse

impulsive

impure

in

inability

inaccuracy

inadvertent/ly

inattention

inaudible

inaugural

incalculable

incapable

incapacitate

incendiary	incompetence
incense	incompetent _or_
incentive	incomplete
inception	inconclusive
incessant	incongruous _or_
inch _or_	inconsiderate
incidence	inconsistency
incident _or_	inconsistent _or_
incidental _or_	inconsolable
incidentally _or_	inconspicuous _or_
inclement	inconstancy
inclination	incontinent
incline	inconvenience
include	inconvenient
inclusive	incorporated _or_
incognito _or_	incorrect
incoherent	increase
income	increasingly
incoming	incredible
incomparable	incredulity
incompatible	increment

incriminate

incubate

incumbent

incur/red /

incurable

indecent or

indeed

indefatigable

indelible

independent/ly /

indescribable

index

index-linked

indication

indicate

indict/able /

indictment

indignant/ly /

indignation or

indispensable

individual or

indolence

indolent

indoors

induce/ment /

indulge

industrial

industrialize

industrious

industry (g)

inefficiency

inefficient/ly /

inequality

inequitable

inevitable

inexorable

inexpensive

inexperience or

inexperienced or

infallible

infect/ion /

infer

inference	injunction ... or
inferior	injure/s ... /
inferiority	injuries
infiltrate	injury
infiltration	ink
inflation	inland
inflict ... or	innocence ... or
influence ... or	innocent
influential	innovate
inform	innovation
informal/ly ... /	innuendo
information	inquest
ingenious	inquire ... or
ingenuous	inquiry
ingrained	inscribe
ingredients	inscription
initial	insect ... or
initiate	insert/ed ... /
initiation	inscrutable
initiative	inside
inject	insignificant

insist	instruct
insistent ... or ...	instruction
insolence ... or ...	instructive
inspect	instructor
inspection	instrument/al ... / ...
inspector	insubordination
inspiration ... or ...	insufficient
inspire ... or ...	insulate
instability	insulation
install	insuperable
installation	insurance
instalment	insure
instance	insurers
instant/ly ... / ...	intelligence
instead ... or ...	intelligent
instigate	intelligible
instinct	intend
instinctive/ly ... / ...	intense
institute	intent
institution	intention
institutional	interest

interfere

interference

interim

intermission

intermittent

internal

international

interpret

interpreter

interrupt/ion

interstate

interval

intervene

intervention

interview

intestate

intimidate

intimidation

into

intolerance

intolerant

intrigue

introduce or

introduction

intruder

intrusion

invasion or

invention

inventive

inventor

inventory

invest

investigate

investigation or

investigator

investment

investors

invigilate

invigilator

invisible

invitation

invite

invoice _(outline)_ or _(outline)_

involve _(outline)_

involvement _(outline)_

inward _(outline)_

irate _(outline)_

iron _(outline)_

irrefutable _(outline)_

irreparable/y _(outline)_ / _(outline)_

irrevocable _(outline)_

irrigate _(outline)_

irrigation _(outline)_

irritate _(outline)_

irritation _(outline)_

is _(outline)_

island _(outline)_

isle _(outline)_

isolate _(outline)_

isolation _(outline)_

issue _(outline)_

it _(outline)_

Italian _(outline)_

italics _(outline)_

itch _(outline)_

item _(outline)_

itself _(outline)_ or _(outline)_

ivory _(outline)_

ivy _(outline)_

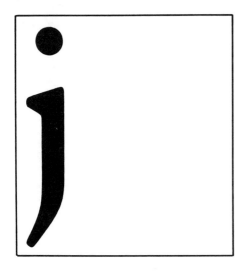

jab

jacket

jade

jam

January

Japanese

jar

jaws

jay

jealous/y

jeans

jeep

jeer

jelly

jersey

jettison

jetty

jewel

jewellery

jibe

jiffy

jive

job

jockey

join

joke

jollity

jolly

jostle

journal

journalist

journey

joy/s

joyous

jubilee

judge		juncture	
judgement		June	
judicial		jungle	
jug		junior	
juice	or	jury	
July		just	
jumble		justice	or
Jumbo jet		justification	
jump/er	/	justify	
junction	or	juvenile	

kale

kedgeree

keen

keep/er /

keepsake

keg

kennel

kept

kerosene

ketch

kettle

key

kick

kid

kidnap

kidney

kill

kiln

kilogram

kilometre

kin

kind/est /

kindle

kindliness

kindly

kindness

kindred

king

kingdom

kingliness

kingly

kingship

kinship

kiss/es /

kissed

kitchen

kitten

knapsack

kneel

knees

knew

knife

knight

knives

knob

knock

know/ing

knowingly

knowledge

knowledgeable

known

laboratory or

label

laboratory

labour/er

lace

lack

laconic

lacquer

ladle

lady

laid

lake

lamb

lame

lament

laugh/able

lamentation

lance

land

landscape

lane

language

lantern

lapse

larceny

large/ly

larger

largest

last

lastly

latch

late/ly

later

latest

latitude

latter/ly

laugh/able

laughter	learn
launch _or_	learner
law	lease _or_
lawful/ly /	leasehold
lawless	least
lawn	leather
lawyer	leave/r /
lax	lecture/r /
lay	led
layers	ledge
layman	leer
lazily	left
laziness	leg
lazy _or_	legacy _or_
lead _or_	legal
leader	legalization
leadership .	legality
leaf	legally
leaflet	legible
leafy	legislation
league	legitimate/ly /

legless	liberation
leisure	liberty
lemon	library
lend	licence _____ or _____
length/en _____ / _____	licensee
lengthy	licenser
less/en _____ / _____	lick
lessee	lie
lesson	life
lessor	lifeless
let	lifespan
lethal	lifetime
letter/s _____ / _____	lift
level	light
levity	light-coloured
liability	lighter
liable	lightning _____ or _____
libel	lightweight
libellous	like/able _____ / _____
liberal/ly _____ / _____	likely
liberality	likeness

likewise	litre
limb/less	little
limit/ed	live
Ltd.	lively
line	liven
linen	liver
liner	livestock
lining	load ... or ...
link	loaf
lion	loan
lip	loath
lip-read	loathe
lipstick	lobby
liquid	lobe
liquidate	lobster
liquidation	local/ly
liquidator	locality
list ... or ...	locate
listen/er	location
literature	lock/er
litigation	locomotion

locomotive

lonely

long

long-distance

longer

longevity

longhand

longing/ly   /

long-term

look/ed   /

look-out   or

loom

loose/n   /

loquacious

lose/r   /

loss

lost

lot   or

lotion

loud   or

lovable

love

lovely

loving/ly   /

low/er   /

loyal/ly   /

loyalty

luck

luckily

lucky

lunch   or

luncheon   or

lung

lush

luxuries

luxurious/ly   /

luxury

lynch   or

machine ....

machinery .... or ....

mad/made .... / ....

magazine ....

magistrate .... or .... (g)

magnanimous ....

magnet .... or ....

magnetic ....

magnetize ....

magneto ....

magnificence ....

magnificent ....

magnify ....

magnitude ....

magnolia ....

magnum ....

maid ....

mail .... or ....

main ....

mainly .... or ....

maintenance ....

majesty ....

major ....

majority ....

make/r .... / ....

male .... or ....

mallet ....

malnutrition ....

mammal ....

man ....

manage ....

management ....

manager ....

manipulate ....

manipulation ....

mankind	masculine	
man-made	mash	
manner	mason	
manpower	mass	
mansion	massive	
manslaughter	master/ly	/
manual	masterpiece	or
manufacture/r	/	mastiff
manuscript	match/less	/
many	mat	
map	mate	
mar	material	
March	maths	
margin/al	/	matter
marine	maxim	
mark/et	/	maximum
marmalade	may	
marriage	mayor	
marry	mayoress	
marshall	maize/maze	/
martial	me	

meadow	memorandum
meagre	memorial
meal	memories
mean	memorize
meant	memory
meantime	men
measure/ment	menace _or_
meat	menagerie
mechanic	mend
mechanical _or_	mention
mechanism	menu/s /
medal	mercantile
media _or_	merchandise
medical	merchant
medicine _or_	mere/ly /
medium	message
meek/ness /	Messrs.
meet	messy
member	met
membership	metal
memoirs	metaphor

meteorological

meteorologist

meteorology

meter

method/ical

metric

metro

metropolitan

Mexican

mice

microfilm

microphone

microprocessing

midday

middle

middle-aged

midnight

Midsummer

might

mike

mile/age

militant

military

milk/man

million

miniature

mince

mind

mindless

mine

miner

minimum

minister

ministry

minority

minute

mirth

mischance

mischief

misdemeanour

mishear

misrepresent

misrepresentation

miss

mission

missionary

mistake

mistaken _or_

mistletoe

misunderstand

misunderstood

mix

mixer

mixture

mob

mobile

mobility

model

moderate

moderation

modern

modernize

modest/ly /

modesty

mohair

moment

momentarily _or_

momentary

monastery

monastic

Monday _or_

monetary

money

monk

monkey

monogram

monopolies

monopolize

monster

month/ly /

moon _or_

mope

moral/morale /

morality

more	much
moreover	mud/dy
morning	muffle
mortgage/e	mug
most	mule
moth	mull
mother/ly	multi-coloured
motion _or_	multifarious
motionless _or_	multi-lateral
motivate	multi-millionaire
motive	multi-racial
motor	multiple
motor bike	multiplication
mottled	multiplicity _or_
move	multiply
movement	multi-storey
mountain	multitude
mouth _or_	multitudinous
mow	munch _or_
Mr.	municipal
Mrs.	municipality

murder ....

murderer ....

muscle .... or ....

museum ....

mushroom ....

music/al .... / ....

must ....

mutton .... or ....

mutual/ly .... / ....

my ....

myself .... or ....

mysterious ....

mystic/al .... / ....

mystified ....

mystify ....

n

nail

name

nameless

namely ... or ...

nape

narrow/ly ... / ...

nation ... or ... (b)

national

nationalization

nationalize

nationality

nationwide

natives

natural/ly ... / ...

nature

naturopath

naturopathic

naturopathy

nave

navigate

navigation

near/by ... / ...

nearly ... or ...

neat/ens ... / ...

neatness

necessarily

necessary

necessity

neck

need

needle

needless

negative

neglect

negligence ... or ...

negligent

negotiate

negotiation

neighbour

neighbourhood

neighbouring

neighbourly

neither

nerves

nervous

nest

net

never .... or ....

nevertheless .... or ....

new

newly

newspaper

newt

New York

next .... or ....

nib

nibble

nice .... or ....

nicely .... or ....

niche

nickel

niece .... or ....

nigh

night/ly .... / ....

nightmare

nine

ninth .... or ....

nip

nipple .... or ....

no

noble

nobly

nobility

noise

noisily

noisy

nonchalant

nondescript	notification
none	notify
nonentities	notion ... or ...
nonentity	notwithstanding
nonsense	nourish/ment ... / ...
non-shrink	novel
non-stop	novice
noon	November
no one	now
nor	nowadays
normal ... or ...	nowhere ... or ...
normality ... or ...	nozzle
normally ... or ...	nudge
north/ern ... / ...	nuisance
nose	numb
not	number ... or ...
notch	numerology
note	numerous
notebook ... or ...	nun
nothing	nunnery
notice ... or ...	nurse

nursery ....

nut ....

nutrition/al .... / ....

nutshell ...... s or ....

nutty ....

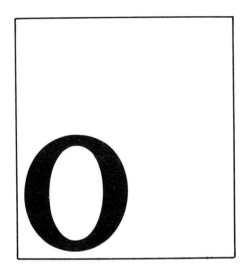

oak

oath

oats

obedience

obey

obituary

object/ion /

objective **or**

obligation

oblige

oblivious

oblong

observance

observation

observe

obsess/ed /

obtain/able /

obtained

obvious

obviously

occasion

occasional/ly /

occupier

occupy

occur

occurrence

ocean

oceanic

o'clock

October

oculist

odd

oddity

of

off

offence	omnibus
offend/er	omnipotent
offer	on/one
offhand	once
office	oneself
officer	onion
official/ly	onlooker
often	only
oh	onset
oil	onto
old/er	onus
oldest	onward
old-established	onyx
old-fashioned	open
olive	open-handed
Olympics	openly
omelette	opera
omen	operate
ominous	operation
omission	operator
omit	opinion

opportunity

opposed

opposite

opposition

optical

optician

optimist

optimistic

optimistically

option/al /

or

oracle

oral

orange

orchard

order/ly /

ordinarily

ordinary

organ

organization

organize

organist

orgy

origin

original/ly /

ornament/al /

ornamentation

orphan

orthodox or

osteopath

osteopathy

other

otherwise

ought

ounce/s /

our

ourselves or

oust

out

outback

outbreak

outcome

outcry	overbearing
outdoor	overboard
outdoors	overcame
outer	overcoat
outfit	overcome
outing	overcrowded
outlay	overdose
outline	overdrive
outlook	overdue
outlying	overfed
output	overflow
outset	overgrown
outside or	overhead
outskirts	overlap
outstanding	overload
outwardly	overlook
outwards	overnight
oval	overpower/ed /
oven	overpowering
over (b) (e)	overprinting
overbalance	override

overrule .... ⟍ᴄ ....

overrun .... ⟋⟋ ....

overseas .... ̆ᵽ ....

oversee .... ̆ᵽ ....

overseer .... ̆ᵽ⟋ ....

overshoes .... ̆ᵴₒ ....

overtake/n .... ⌣ᴢ / ⌣ᴛ ....

overtime .... ⌣ᴢ ....

overtook .... ⌣⟍ᴄ ....

overwhelm .... ⌣ᴛ ....

owe/owing .... ⌣ / ⌣⟋ ....

own/ed .... ⟍⟋ / ⌣ᴛ ....

owner .... ⟍⟋ ....

ox .... ⤬ ....

oxen .... ⤬l ....

oxygen .... ⤬⟋ or ⤬⟋ ....

pack	pall
package	palm
packet	pamphlet
padre	pan
page ... or	pandemonium
paid	panel
pain/ful /	pant
painless	pantry
paint/er /	paper
pairs	paradise
pal	parallel
palate	parcel ... or
palatial ... or	parent/al /
pale	parity

park

Parliament

parliamentary

parrot

parson

part/ly /

partial/ly /

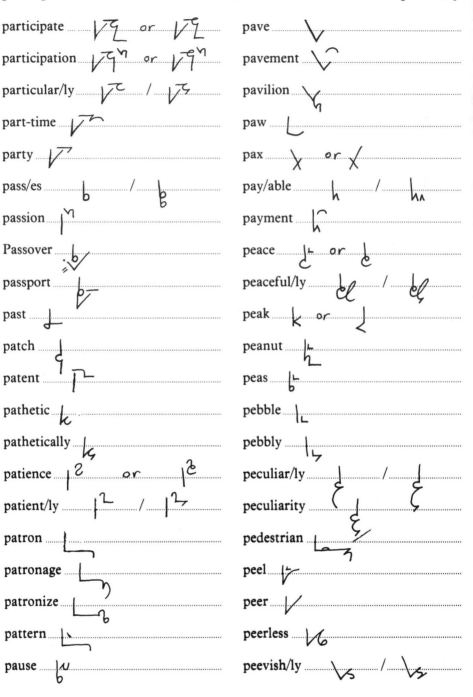

participate	pave
participation	pavement
particular/ly	pavilion
part-time	paw
party	pax ... or
pass/es	pay/able
passion	payment
Passover	peace ... or
passport	peaceful/ly
past	peak ... or
patch	peanut
patent	peas
pathetic	pebble
pathetically	pebbly
patience ... or	peculiar/ly
patient/ly	peculiarity
patron	pedestrian
patronage	peel
patronize	peer
pattern	peerless
pause	peevish/ly

peg		performer	
pen		perfume	
pence	or (g)	perhaps	
pencil		period	
pending		periodical/ly	/
penetrate		permanent/ly	/
penetration		permission	
penitence		permit	
pension/able	/	persecute	or
pensioner		persecution	or
people		perseverance	
pepper		persevere	
perceive		persist	or
per cent		persistence	or
percentage		persistent	or
perceptible		person	
perfect		personal/ly	/
perfection		personality	
perfectly		personnel	
perforation		perspective	
perform/ance	/	persuade	

persuasion		pianist	
pertaining		piano	
pet	or	pick	
petition		picket	or
petitioner		pickle	
petrol	or	picnic	
petroleum	or	picture	
phase	or	picturesque	
phial		pie	
phone	or	piece	or
photo		pier	
photograph/er	/	pig	
photographic		pigeon	
photography		pile	
phrase/s	/	pill	
physical		pin	
physics		pinch	or
physiological		pink	
physiology		pint	
physiotherapist		pipe	
physiotherapy		pitch	

pith		
pivot		
pixie		
place	or	
placid	or	
plain/ly	/	
plaintiff		
plan		
plane		
planner		
plant		
plantation		
plate		
plateau	or	
plateful		
platinum	or	
plausible		
play/er	/	
playground		
plea		
plead	or	

pleasant/ly	/	
please		
pleasurable		
pleasure		
plentiful		
plenty		
plight		
plough		
pluck		
plucky		
plunge		
plus	or	
plywood		
pocket		
poem		
poetry		
point/less	/	
poison/s	/	
poisonous		
police		
policeman		

policy	porter
polish	portfolio ... or ...
political	portion
politician	position
politics	positive/ly ... / ...
pollen	possess/ion ... / ...
pollinate	possible
pollute	possibility
pollution	possibly
pond	post
ponder/s ... / ...	postage
ponderous	postal
pony	postal order ... or ...
pool	poster
poor/ly ... / ...	posterity
poorest	posthumous
pop	post-mortem
popular	post office ... or ...
popularity	postpone
population	pot
port/able ... / ...	potato

potent	predict/able ... /
pottery ... or	predictably
pound	prediction
poverty	predominate
powder	prefabricated
power	preface ... or
powerful	prefer/ence ... /
powerfully	prejudge
powerless	prejudice ... or
practicable	preliminary ... or
practical/ly ... /	premature
practice ... or	premises
practise ... or	premium
practitioner	pre-packed
pray	preparation
preach	prepare
preacher	prescribe ... or
precaution ... or	prescription ... or
precious ... or	present
precise/ly ... /	presentation
precision ... or	presenter

presently	Prime Minister
present time	prince/s
preservation	princess
preserve	principal/principle
preside	print/er
president/ial	print-out ... or
press	prior
pressure	priority
Prestel	prison/er
prestige	private/ly
presume	privilege
pretty	prize ... or
prevalence	prizes ... or
prevalent	probability
prevent	probable
prevention	probably
previous/ly	probate
price ... or	probation/er
price list	problem
pride	procedure
prime	proceed/ings

process/es	prolong
procession	promenade
processor	prominence
prod	prominent/ly
prodigal	promise
prodigality	promote/r
produce	promotion
product/ion	prompt/ly
productive	pronounce
productivity	pronunciation
profess	proof
profession	propaganda
professional	proper/ly
proficient	property
profit/able	proportion
pro-forma	proportionate/ly
programme/r	proposal
progress/ion	propose
prohibit/ion	proposition
project	proprietor
prologue	propriety

prose

prosecute ... or ...

prosecution ... or ...

prospect

prospective

prosper

prosperity

prosperous

protect/ion ... / ...

protective

protein

protest

protestation

proud/ly ... / ...

prove

proven

proverb

proverbial

provide

provisions

proximity

proxy

prudence

prudent/ly ... / ...

psychiatric

psychiatrist

psychiatry

psychological

psychologist

psychology

psychopath

psychopathic

public

publication

publicity

publicize ... or ...

publish

publisher

pudding

puff

pull

pullet

pummel

pump

puncture

punish/ment .... /

pupil

purchase

pure/ly .... /

purest

purpose/ly .... /

purse

pursue

push

put .... or

putty .... or

puzzle

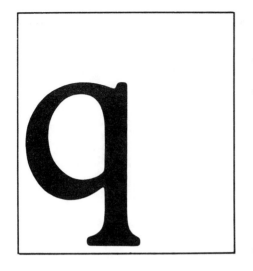

quarterly

queen

query

quest

question ... or ...

questionable ... or ...

queue/d ... / ...

quack

quibble

quaff ... or ...

quick ... or ...

quail

quickly ... or ...

quake

quid

qualifications

quiet/ly ... / ...

qualified

quip

qualify ... or ... or ...

quill

quality

quince

qualm

quire

quantity

quirk

quarantine

quit

quarrel

quite

quarry

quiver

quarter ... or ... (g)

quiz

quorum

quotation

quote or

ragged

rail

railway/s

rain

rainfall

raise

rake

rabbit

race ... or ...

racial

rack

radar

radiation

radical

radically ... or ...

radio

radiogram

radiographer

radiologist

radiology

radium

rally

ran

rang

range

rank

rapid

rare/ly ... / ...

rarity

rash/ly ... / ...

rashness

rat

rate/able ... / ...

ratepayer

rather ... or ...

ration	realm	
rational	reason/able	
rave	reasonably	
raw	rebel/s	
ray/s	rebound	
raze	recall	
razor _or_	receipt _or_	
reach	receive _or_	
react/ion	recent	
read/able	recently _or_	
reader	reception	
readily	receptionist	
readiness	receptive	
ready	receptivity	
real	recession	
realism	recipe	
realistic	recital	
reality	recite	
realize	recognition	
realizing	recognizance	
really	recognize	

recommend ___ or ___

recommendation ___

recompense ___ or ___

record ___

recover/y ___ / ___

recruit ___

recur/rence ___ / ___

red ___

redeem/er ___ / ___

redemption ___

redevelop/ment ___ / ___

reduce ___ or ___

reduction ___

redundancy/cies ___ / ___

reef ___

refer ___

referee ___

reference ___

referendum ___ or ___

refine ___

reflect/ion ___ / ___

reform ___

reformation ___

refrain ___

refresh ___

refreshment ___

refuge ___

refugee ___

refund ___

refusal ___

refuse ___

regal ___

regard ___

regiment ___

regimentation ___

region/al ___ / ___

register ___

registrar ___

registration ___

registry ___

regret ___

regular/ly ___ / ___

reign/rein

reinvest

reinvestment

reject/ed

rejoice   or

relate

relations

relationship

relative/ly

relax/ation

release

relent/less

relevant

reliable

reliability

reliably

religion

religious   or

rely

remain

remainder

remake

remark/able

remedies

remedy

remember

remind/er

remit/tance

remonstrance

remonstrate

removable   or

remove   or

render   or

renew/al

rent

repair

repent/ance

repercussions

repetition

repetitive

replace/ment

replay

reply

report/er   /

reprehensible

represent   or

representation

representative

repress/ion   /

reprieve

reprimand

reprint

reprisal   or

reproach/ful   /

reproduce   or

reproduction   or

republic/an   /

repugnance

reputable

reputation

request

requiem

require   or

requirement

requisite

requisition

research

rescue

resemblance

resemble

resent/ful   /

resign

resignation   or

resist/ance   /

resolution

resources

respect

respectful/ly   /

respective/ly   /

respond

response

responsible

responsibility

rest/ful   /

restless/ness

restaurant

restitution

restive

restoration

restore

restrain

restraint

result

resume

resumption

retail/er

retain/er

retire/ment

retrain

retrospect/ive

retrieve

retriever

return

revelation

revenge

revenue

reverse

review

revise

revision

revival

revive

revolution/ary

revolutionize

revolve

revolver

reward

rhyme

rhythm

ribbon

rice

rich

ride

ridicule

ridiculous

riddle

rife		romp	
rift	or	roof	or
right		room/y	/
right-hand		roost	
rim		roots	or
ring		rope	
rise/n	/	rose	
risk		rosy	or
rival		rot	
river		rotate	
road		rotation	
roar		rough/ly	/
robin		round/ly	/
rock		routine	or
rockery		rove	
rode		row	
rogue		royal/ty	/
roll/er	/	rub	
Roman		rubber	
romance		rubbish	
romantic		rubble	

rug

rule/r   /

rumours

run

rung

rural

rush

rush-hour

Russian   or

rust/y   /

salt

salutary

same

sample

sampler

sand

sandal

sang

sank

sash ... or

sat

satin

satisfaction

satisfactorily

satisfactory

satisfy

Saturday ... or

saturate/d ... /

saturation

savage

save

sacrilege

sad/ly ... /

saddle

safe/ty ... /

safeguard

sago

said

sail/sale

sailor

salaries

salary

saleable

salesman ... or

salient

savings

saviour

savour

saw

say/s

scab

scale

scandal/s

scandalous

scar/scare

scene

scenery

sceptic/al

schedule

scheme

scholar

scholarship

school

schoolboy

science _or_

scientific _or_

scientifically _or_

scientist _or_

scissors _or_

scorpion

Scottish

scratch _or_

screen _or_

screw

scrounge/r

sea

seaside

season

seat

seaward

second _or_ (g)

secondary

secondly

second-class

second-hand

secret

secretarial

secretary	self-evident	
secretly	selfish	
section	selfishly	
sector	self-possessed	
secure	self-propelled	
securities	self-reliant	
security	self-satisfied	
see/ing	self-service	
seed	self-supporting	
seek	self-willed	
seem	sell/er	
seemingly	semiautomatic	
seen	semicircle	
select/ion	semicircular	
selective	semicolon	
self-confidence	semiconscious	
self-contained	semidarkness	
self-control	semi-detached	
self-defence	semiprecious	
self-denial	semitropical	
self-employed	send	

senile

senility

senior/ity

sensation

sense/less

sensibility

sensible

sensibly

sensitive/ly

sensitivity

sent

sentence

sentiment

sentimental

sentimentality

separate/ly

separation

September

sequence

serene   or

serenity

serial

series

serious

seriously   or

seriousness

sermon

servant

serve

service   or

servile

session

set

settle/ment

seven

seventh

several

severe

severity

sew

sex

sexual

sexuality	sharply ... or
shabby	sharpness
shade	shatter
shadow/y /	shave
shady	shawl
shaft	she
shaggy	sheaf
shake	shear
shaken	shed
shall	sheep
shallow	sheet
shambles	shelf ... or
shame	shell ... or
shameful ... or	shellfish ... or
shameless	shepherd
shape/ly /	sheriff
share	sherry
shareholders	shine
shark	ship/ment /
sharp	shirt
sharpen/ed /	shock/ed /

shoe

shop

shopkeeper

shoplifting

shopper

short/age

shorter

shortest

shorthand ... or ...

shorthand-typist

shortly

shot ... or ...

should

shoulders

shout

shovel

show

shown

shrewd

shriek/ed ... / ...

shrill

shrimp

shrink

shrub

shunt

shut

shuttle

shy ... or ...

sick

sicken/ing ... / ...

side ... or ...

sideboard

sieve

sigh/s ... / ...

sight

sign

signal

signature

significance

significant/ly ... / ...

signpost

silence/r ... / ...

silent/ly	/	situation or
silicon		six/ty /
silk		sixteen
silver/y	/	size or
similar	or	skate
similarly	or	sketch
similarity		skill
simple		skin
simplicity	or	skirt
simply		sky
since	or	slander
sincere	or	slave/ry /
sincerely	or (g)	slavish/ly /
sing/er	/	slice or
single		slide
singly		slight
sink		slightest
sir		slightly or
sister		slim/mer /
sit		slip/pery /
site		slope

slow/er	/	so
slowest		soak
slowly		soap
sluggish		sob/s /
small or		sober
smaller or		social
smallest or		socialism
smallpox		socialist
smart/er /		society or
smartest		sociological
smash		sociologist
smell		sociology
smile		sock
smoke/r /		soft
smooth		softens
snack		softness
snag		sold
snake or		soldier
snap		solid or
sneeze		solemn
snow		solicitor or

solitary	sort
solo	sought
soluble	soul _or_
solution _or_	sound
solve	soup _or_
solvency	source _or_
solvent	south
some	southern
someone	sow
somehow	space _or_
something	spade
sometimes	span
somewhere	spanner
son	spare
song	sparse
soon _or_	speak/er _or_ /
soothe	special/ly /
sophisticated	specialist
sophistication	speciality
sorrow	specimen
sorry	spectators

speech	spot
speed/ily /	spotless
speedy	spout
spell	spray
spend	spread
spent	spring
spin	spur
spirit	spurious
spite	spy
spiteful/ly /	squadron
spitefulness	squander
splash	square/ly /
splendid/ly /	squat
splendour	squatter
split	squirrel
spoke/n or /	stability or
spokesman	stable
sponsor	stage
spoon	stamp
sport	stand
sportsman/woman /	standard

star		still	
start		stimulate	
state/ment	/	stimulation	
statesman/men	/	stitch	
station	or	stock	
stationary	or	stock market	
stationery	or	stone	
statistical		stony	
statistics		stomach	
stay		stood	
steam		stop/page	/
steal/steel		storage	
stem		store/s	/
stenographer		story	
stenography		storm/y	/
step		straightforward	
stern		strange/ly	/
stick		stranger/est	/
stiff		strategic	
stiffen		strategically	
stiffer		strategy	

strawberry/ies	subdue
strength/en	sub-editor ... or
stress	subject/ion
stretch	subjective
strict/ly	submit ... or
stride	subscribe
strike	subscriber
string	subscription
strong/er	subsequent/ly
strongly	subservience
structure	subservient
struggle	subside
strung	subsidence
stubble	subsidiary
student	subsoil
studied	substance
studio	substantial ... or
study	substantially ... or
stuff	substantiate
stupid/ly	suburbs
subdivide	subzero ... or

success

successful/ly /

succession

successive

such or

suck

sudden/ly /

sue/d /

suede

suffer/ed /

sufficiency

sufficient

sufficiently

sugar

suggest/ion /

suggestive

suit/suite

suitable

suitor

sultry

sum

summary

summer/y /

sun

Sunday or

sung

sunlight

sunshine

super or (b)

superannuation

superb/ly /

superficial

superficially

superfluous

superhuman

superintend/ent /

superior/ity /

supermarket

supernatural

supersede

supersonic

superstition

superstitious	surprise
supervise	surreptitious
supervision	surroundings
supervisor	survey/or /
supper	susceptible
supple	suspect
supplement	suspicion
supplementary	suspicious/ly /
supplies	sustain
supply	swam
support/ers /	sway
supportive	sweet/ly /
suppose	swell or
supposed	swim
supposition	swimmer
sure/ly /	swing
surf	switch
surface or	switch-over
surge	swung
surgery	syllable
surplus	syllabus

symbol/ic   /

sympathetic

sympathetically

sympathy

symptoms

synonymous

synthetic   or

system

systematic

systematically

table/s .... / ....

tabulate ....

tabulator ....

tackle ....

tact ....

tactful/ly .... / ....

tactless ....

tadpoles ....

tail ....

take ....

taken .... or ....

takeover ....

talk ....

talkative ....

tale ....

tall ....

tamper ....

tan ....

tangible ....

tangle ....

tank/er .... / ....

tannin ....

tanning ....

tap ....

tariff/s .... / ....

tarnish ....

task ....

taste ....

tasty ....

tattoo ....

tax .... or ....

taxation .... or ....

tax-free ....

taxi .... or ....

tea ....

teach/er	telephone
teak	telephonist
team	telescope
tear	telescopic
tease	television ... or
teaspoon	telex
tea-time	tell
technical	temerity
technological ... or	temper
technology ... or	temperament/al ... /
tedious	ten
Teeline	tenable
teenage/r ... /	tenant
teens	tend
teeth	tendency
telecommunications	tennis
telegram	tension
telegraph	tent
telegraphy	term
telepathic	terminal
telepathy	termination

terrace .... or ....

terrible ....

terribly ....

territory ....

terror ....

terrorist ....

terrorize ....

test ....

testament ....

text .... or ....

than ....

thank ....

thankful/ly .... / ....

thankfulness .... or ....

thankless ....

thanklessness ....

that ....

thatch ....

thaw ....

the ....

theatre .... or ....

theatrical ....

theft ....

their ....

them ....

theme ....

themselves .... or ....

then ....

thence ....

theoretical ....

theory ....

therapist .... or ....

therapy .... or .... (e)

there .... or ....

thereafter ....

thereby ....

therefore ....

therm ....

Thermos ....

these ....

thesis ....

they ....

thick/en

thicker

thickly

thief

thieves

thigh

thin

thing ... or ... (g)

things ... or ... (g)

think/er

third ... or ... (g)

thirst/y

thirty

this

thistle

thong

thorough/ly

those

though

thought

thoughtful/ly

thoughtfulness

thoughtless

thoughtlessness

thousand ... or ... (g)

thread

threat

threaten/ed

three

threw

thrift/y

thrill

thrive

thriving

throat

throb

through ... or ...

throughout ... or ...

throw/n

thrush

thrust

thumb

thunder	tireless
Thursday ... or	title
thus	to
ticket	toast
tickle	tobacco
tide	today
tidy	toe
tie	together ... or
tiger	token ... or
tight/ly ... /	tolerant
tiles	tolerate
till	toleration
timber	told
time	tomato
time-table	tomorrow ... or
tin	tongue
tinker	ton/tonne
tiny	tonnage
tinny	tonight
tip	too
tire/d ... /	took

tool	trade/r
toolkit	tradesman/men
tooth	tradition *or*
toothache	traditional/ly
top	traffic
topical	train
torrent/ial	trainee
tortoise	trance
toss	tranquil/lity
total/ly	tranquillizers
touch	transact/ion
tough	transcribe
tour/ist	transcript/ion
towards	transfer/ence
tower	transform/ation
town	transistor
toy	transitory
trace *or*	translate
track	translation
tract	translator
tractor	transmission

transmit/ter _____ / _____

transpire _____

transplant _____

transport/er _____ / _____

trans-ship _____

trans-shipment _____

travel/ler _____ / _____

travelling _____

tray/s _____ / _____

tread _____

treasure/r _____ / _____

treat/ment _____ / _____

treble/trebly _____ / _____

tree/s _____ / _____

trek _____

tremendous/ly _____ / _____

trench _____ or _____

trend/y _____ / _____

trial _____

tribe _____

tribute _____

trick _____

tried _____

trip _____

tropical _____

trouble _____ or _____

troubled _____ or _____

trough _____

trousers _____ or _____

truant _____ or _____

truck _____

true/truly _____ / _____

trunk _____

trust/ee _____ / _____

truth _____

truthful _____ or _____

truthfully _____ or _____

try/ing _____ / _____

tuck _____

Tuesday _____ or _____

tuft _____

tug _____

tuition

tulip

tumour

turkey

turn

turnover

turtle

tutors

TV

twelve

twice _or_

twin

twist

two

type

typical

typing

typist

typewriter

u

ugly

ulcer _____ or _____

ultramodern

ultraviolet

ultimate

ultimatum

umbrella

umpire

unable

unaccompanied

unalterable

unanimous

unbiased

unceasing

uncertain/ly _____ / _____

uncertainty

uncle _____ or _____

uncomfortable

uncommon

uncommunicative

uncomplicated

uncomplimentary

unconcerned _____ or _____

unconscious

unconstitutional

uncontaminated

uncontrollable

under _____ (b)

undergo

undergone

underhand

underinsured

underlying

undermine

underpass

underprivileged

understand

understood

understudy

undertake/n

undertook

underwriter

undo

undoubted/ly

uneconomic

uneconomical

unemployed

unemployment

unexpected/ly

unfinished

unfortunate/ly

uniform

union

uninsured

unique

unit/unite

universal

university/ies

unknowingly

unknown

unless

unlikely

unlucky

unnecessary

unofficial/ly

unprepared

unproductive

unquestionably

unruffled

unseasonal

unseasonable

unscrupulous

unsympathetic

untangle

until

unusual/ly

unwanted

unwary	urban
unwelcome	urchin
unwell	urge .... or ....
unwilling/ly .... /	urgency
up	urgent/ly .... / ....
upkeep	us
upon	usable
upper ....(b)	usage
upper case	use
upper class	useful/ly .... / ....
upper hand	useless
upper house	usual/ly .... / ....
uppermost	usurp
upper storey	utility
upright	utilize
uproar	utmost
uproot/ing .... /	utter
upset	utterance
upside	utterly
upward/s .... /	uttermost

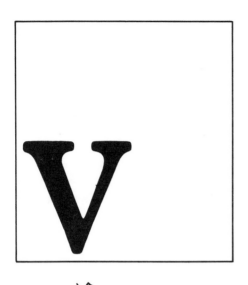

value

valve

van

vandalism

vandals

vanish

vanity

vantage

vapour

variable

varies   or

variety

various

vary

vase

vast

vault

vegetable/s   /

veer/ed   /

vehemence

vehicle

vacancy

vacant

vacate

vacation

vaccinate

vaccination

vaccine

vague

vain/ly   /

vale   or

valiant

valid

valley

valuable/ation   /

veins	vestments
velvet	veteran ... or
ventilate	vex/ed ... /
ventilator	via
ventriloquist	viable
venture	vicar
venue	vice ... or
verbatim	victim
verdict	victimization
verge/r ... /	victimize
verification	vie/d ... /
verify ... or	view/er ... /
verity	vigilance
versatile	vigilant
versatility	vigour
verse	village
versus	vim
vertical	vindicate
very	vindictive
vessel	vinegar
vest	vintage

violate

violation

violence

violent

violin

virtue/s /

virtuous

virus

visa

visible

visibly

visibility

vision

visionary

visit/ors /

visual

visualized

vital

vitamin

vivid

vixen

vocabulary

vocal

vogue

voice or

void

volcano

volts

voltage

voluble

volubly

volume

voluntary

volunteer

vote/r /

vouch/er /

vowels

vulgar/ity /

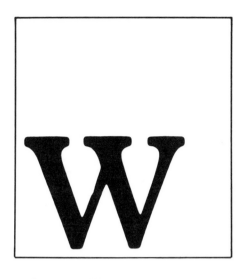

walnut   or

waltz

wander/er   /

wandering

want

wanton

war

ward   or   (e)

warden

warder

warehouse

wares

warm/er   /

warmly   or

warmth

warn/ed   /

warrant

warrior

warship

was

wash/es   /

wade

wafer

waffle

waft/ed   /

wage/r   /

wagon

waist

wait

wake/n   /

walk   or

walkabout

walker

wall

wallet

washer

wasp

waste

wasteful/ness

watch/ers

watchful/ness

water/y

wave

waver

wax

waxworks

way

wayside

we

weak/er

weakness

wealth/y

weapon

wear/ing

weariness

weary

weather

weave

weaving

web

wedding

wedge

Wednesday   or

weed

week

weekend

weep

weigh/ed

weight/y

welcome

welfare

well

well-being   or

well-educated

well-groomed

well-known

well-off

well-planned

went

were

west/ern

westward

wet

whale _or_

what

whatever

wheel

when

whenever _or_

where

whereas

wherein

whereupon

whether

which _or_

whichever _or_

while/whilst

whim

whip

whisk _or_

whisker

whisky

whisper

whist

whistle _or_

white

Whitehall

whiting

Whitsun

who

whole _or_

wholemeal _or_

wholesale/r

wholly

whom

whose

why

wide/ly

widow

wife	wit
wig	with
wild	withdraw/n
will	wither
willing/ly	within
win	or	without	or
wince	witness/ed
wind	witnesses
windmill	witty
window	wizard
windy	wobble
wine	wobbly
wing	woe
winner	woke
winter	woman
wipe	or	womb
wiper	or	women
wire	won
wisdom	wonder
wise	wonderful/ly
wish/ful	woo	or

woods

wool

woollen

word ...... or ...... (e/g)

word-processing

word-processor

wore

work/er ...... / ......

workman/men ...... / ......

workshop

world

world-wide

worm

worried

worries

worry

worse

worship

worst

worth/less ...... / ......

worthy

would ...... or ...... (g)

wound

wrangle

wrap

wrapper

wreck/age ...... / ......

wretch

wring

writ

write/r ...... / ......

written

wrong/ly ...... / ......

wrote

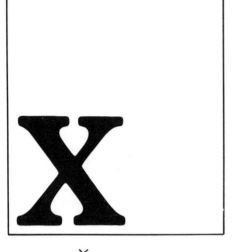

Xerox

x-ray

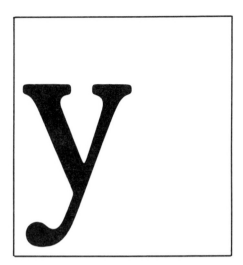

yesterday

yesteryear

yet

yield

yodel

yoga

yoghurt

yoke

yokel

you

young/er   /

youngest

youngster

your

yourself/ves   /

youth

youthful

yacht

yale

yard

year/ly   /

yeast

yell

yellow

yelp

yeoman

yes

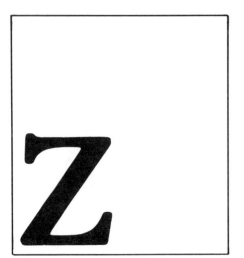

zero

zest

zigzag

zip

zither

zodiac

zone

zoo

zoom

zoologist

zoology

zany

zeal

zebra

zenith

APPENDIX 1   Countries

Afghanistan

Albania

Algeria

America

Angola

Argentina

Australia

Austria

Bangladesh

Belgium

Bolivia

Botswana

Brazil ...... or ......

Bulgaria

Burma

Canada

Chile

China

Colombia

Costa Rica

Cuba

Cyprus

Czechoslovakia

Denmark

Dominican Republic

Ecuador

Egypt

England

Ethiopia

Finland

France

Germany

Ghana

Greece ...... or ......

Greenland

Guatemala

Haiti

Holland

Honduras

Hong Kong

Hungary

Iceland

India

Indonesia

Iran

Iraq

Ireland

Israel

Italy

Jamaica

Japan

Jordan

Kenya

Korea

Kuwait

Laos

Lebanon

Liberia

Libya

Luxembourg

Malawi

Malaysia

Malta

Mauritius

Mexico

Mongolia

Morocco

Mozambique

Namibia

Nepal

Netherlands

New Zealand

Nicaragua

Nigeria

Norway

Pakistan

Panama

Paraguay

Peru

Philippines

Poland

Portugal

Romania

Russia

Saudi Arabia

Scotland

Sierra Leone

Singapore

South Africa

Spain

Sri Lanka

Sudan

Sweden

Switzerland

Syria

Taiwan

Tanzania

Tasmania

Thailand

Trinidad

Tunisia

Turkey

Uganda

U.K.

United Kingdom

United States

Uruguay

U.S.A.

U.S.S.R.

Venezuela

Vietnam

Wales

Yugoslavia

Zaïre

Zambia

Zimbabwe

APPENDIX 2   Towns and Cities

United Kingdom

Aberdeen	Fishguard
Aberystwyth	Glasgow
Belfast	Gloucester
Birmingham	Holyhead
Blackpool	Hull
Bournemouth	Inverness
Brighton	Kendal
Bristol	Lancaster
Buxton	Leeds
Cambridge	Leicester
Canterbury	Lincoln
Cardiff	Liverpool
Carlisle	London
Darlington	Manchester
Dover	Newcastle-upon-Tyne
Durham	Northampton
Edinburgh	Norwich
Exeter	Nottingham
	Oban
	Oxford

Plymouth

Portsmouth

Scarborough

Sheffield

Shrewsbury

Southampton

Stranraer

Swansea

Truro

York

Australia

Adelaide

Brisbane

Canberra

Darwin

Geelong

Melbourne

Perth

Surfers Paradise

Sydney

Whyalla

Wollongong

Tasmania

Hobart

Canada

Calgary

Edmonton

Gander

Halifax

Montreal

Quebec

Toronto

Vancouver

Winnipeg

New Zealand

Auckland

Christchurch

Dunedin

Hamilton

Queenstown

Wanganui

Wellington

U.S.A.

Boston

Chicago

Cincinnati

Detroit

Los Angeles

Minneapolis

New York

San Francisco

Washington

European capitals

Athens

Berlin

Bonn

Copenhagen

Helsinki

Lisbon

Madrid

Moscow

Oslo

Paris

Rome

Stockholm

Vienna

Warsaw

APPENDIX 3   Additional Words

abrupt

accent

acrylic ... or

acupuncture

aerobics ... or

affidavit ... or

affray

airborne

alignment

ambidextrous

ambiguity

ambivalent

amphetamine ... or

anaemia

anaesthetic

anchor

antifreeze

aperture

apology ... or

apostrophe ... or

arithmetic

articulate

aspiration

aspire

assets ... or

assignment

athletic

attorney

aubergine

auspicious

authentic

autistic

babysitter

backdated

bacteria

barbecue

baritone

barometer

barrister

bicycle		
bikini		
blouse		
bluff		
boutique		
breathalyser		
breathtaking		
Britain		
browse		
brusque		
butterfly	or	
cafeteria		
caftan	or	
calculator	or	
calendar		
cameo		
canine		
cardboard		
carefree		
carton		

cartoon	or	
casino		
cassette	or	
caterer		
catering		
cattle		
Ceefax		
celebrity		
cellulose		
census		
chalet		
championship		
chassis		
chastise		
checklist		
chipolata		
chlorophyll	or	
complexity	or	
component		
conclusion		
confectioner		

confectionery	dessert
congress	detector
consortium _or_	devastate
continuity	device
correspondent	devise
cosmetics	digital
cosmonaut	diminish _or_
credibility	diminishing _or_
credit card _or_	discotheque
creditworthy	dishwasher
criteria	disillusioned
crumple	dissolve
curio	domino
curriculum	donkey
cursor	downstream
	drought
daisywheel	duet
data	duration
daybreak	duty-free
denims	dynamo
departmental _or_	dyslexia

dyslexic

earn

earnings

earthly ... or ...

echo

effluent

élite ... or ...

emigrate

ended

endorsement

endowment

enlightenment

entail

enumerator

erase ... or ...

escalator

ethical

ethnic

expertise

extempore ... or ...

facsimile ... or ...

fanbelt

fantastic

felon

flamboyant

flown ... or ...

fluoride

foible

forecourt

forename

forever

format

formula

forthright

fox ... or ...

franchise

fraudulent

freezer

frequency

friction

frisky

fullstop		headlong		
fuse		headset		
		herald		
gazeteer		hero		
gazetted		hideous	*or*	
genes		highway		
genius		hi-tech		
geriatric		hoax	*or*	
glue		homophone	*or*	
goulash		hormone		
graze		horrendous	*or*	
guerilla		hostage		
guidelines		hostess		
guillotine		housebound		
guitar		hovercraft		
		humidity		
hallucination		hydrofoil	*or*	
halo	*or*	hypermarket		
hardware				
hare		idiosyncracy		
haughty		impact		

inarticulate

incautious

indices   or

indifferent

indisposed

infamous   or

inherit

input

intact

integrate

integrity

intercom

intermediate

Interpol   or

inverted

ironic

irregularity

irresistible   or

itemize

Jobcentre

keyboard

laminated

lasagne

laser

lateral

lathe

left-handed

lettuce

lever

licentiate

lifestyle

likelihood

localize

loft

logo

loudspeaker

lucrative   or

lunchtime

magic

manilla

marina

marketable

marketing

marzipan ... or

melon ... or

mercenary

mesh

messenger

metamorphosis ... or

metre

metrication

microchip

micro-electronics

microfiche ... or

millilitre

millimetre

minestrone

misled

modify

module

molecular

molecule

monitored

moodiness ... or

motherhood

motorway

motto

muscular

naval

nectarine

network

newsagent

notorious

nuclear

numerate

obstruction

offshore

Ombudsman

onshore

Oriental
orienteering
osmosis
outrageous
overdraft
overdrawn
overtype
overweight

pantomime
paper-clip
parameter
pasta
paté
patio
peripatetic
peripheral
permissive
Perspex
phenomena
phonetics
photocopier
photostat
pica
pilot
pioneer
piteous
piteously
pizza
plastic
playgroup
plural
polyester
polyglot
polygon
polyurethane
postcode
potential
pound (weight or verb)
prepaid
prettier
prettiest

proof-read

proprietary

prospects

prospectus

prototype — or —

psychedelic

punch

punched

quango

quartz

questionnaire — or —

quiche

radius

railroad

ramification

random

ratio

ravioli

rebuilding

recess — or —

reciprocal

reconcile

recycled

rediffusion — or —

regardless

rehearsal

rehearse

reimburse

reinforce

relegate

renegade — or —

reptile

retractable

retrieval

riverside

rodent

rudimentary

sacrifice — or —

salutation

satellite _(outline)_ or _(outline)_	shredder _(outline)_
sauna _(outline)_	shrinkage _(outline)_
sausage _(outline)_	shrugged _(outline)_
scaffolding _(outline)_ or _(outline)_	silo _(outline)_ or _(outline)_
scampi _(outline)_	singular _(outline)_ or _(outline)_
scarcity _(outline)_	slapdash _(outline)_
score _(outline)_	slipshod _(outline)_
script _(outline)_ or _(outline)_	socio-economic _(outline)_
search _(outline)_	socket _(outline)_
seasonal _(outline)_	software _(outline)_
seatbelt _(outline)_	soprano _(outline)_
segregate _(outline)_	sovereign _(outline)_
seminar _(outline)_	spaghetti _(outline)_
sequential _(outline)_	specifically _(outline)_ or _(outline)_
sewage _(outline)_	sprint _(outline)_
sheath _(outline)_	squeamish _(outline)_
sheaves _(outline)_	squeeze _(outline)_
shield _(outline)_ or _(outline)_	stamina _(outline)_
shift _(outline)_	stapler _(outline)_
shiver _(outline)_	stifle _(outline)_
shrank _(outline)_	stipulate _(outline)_

strictest

striped

stubborn

submarine   or

substitute

subtle

suburban

succeed

sunset

supertax

supplier

surname

suspension

swan

sweetheart

swerve

swimwear

tachograph   or

takeaway

tally

technique

telemessage

Teletext   or

Terylene

texture   or

thermal   or

thumbnail

tort

toxic   or

transit

transpose

trolley

tutorial

unbroken   or

unclear

unflattering   or

unload

unorthodox

unpredictable

unsure

untidy

unused

unwieldy

unwillingness

unzip

upholstery

upstairs

vanilla

vending

veto

video　　　or

villain　　or

vinyl

vocational

wharf

wharves

whereby

wherewithal　　or

workforce

workmanship

yawn